THE DEATH OF LORD NELSON

PUBLISHER'S NOTE

The frontispiece (*see page 85*) showing Lord
Nelson in the battle dress which he was wearing
when he received his fatal wound, together with
the title page (*see page 90*), are facsimiles from the
original edition published by T. Cadell and W.
Davies, London, 1807.

The plate reproduced on page 70 depicting
engravings of the actual musket ball which
mortally wounded His Lordship is also
reproduced from the same edition. The upper
illustration shows the musket ball, in the exact
state in which it was extracted by Mr Beatty,
with a portion of the gold-lace and pad of the
epaulette and also a piece of His Lordship's
coat, firmly attached. The lower illustration
shows the clasp containing the fatal ball
mounted in crystal as presented to Mr Beatty by
Sir Thomas Hardy. This clasp subsequently
joined Her Majesty Queen Victoria's Collection
in the Armoury at Windsor Castle.

Mr Beatty was appointed Physician to the Fleet
at the Royal Naval Hospital Greenwich
(1806–40) and received a knighthood in 1831.

THE DEATH OF LORD NELSON

THE AUTHENTIC NARRATIVE

With the circumstances preceding, attending,
and subsequent to that event; the Professional
Report on His Lordship's Wound; and several
interesting anecdotes

By

WILLIAM BEATTY M.D.

Surgeon to the Victory in the
Battle of Trafalgar

Foreword by

REAR ADMIRAL
CHARLES WESTON C.B.

THE ATHENAEUM
PUBLISHING COMPANY LTD

FOURTH EDITION

THE ATHENAEUM PUBLISHING COMPANY LTD 1985

Design and Foreword this edition, Copyright © 1985
The Athenaeum Publishing Company Ltd

ISBN 0 9510370 05   PAPERBACK

Distributed by Stobart & Son Ltd,
67–73 Worship Street, London EC2A 2EL

British Library Cataloguing in Publication Data

Beatty, *Sir* William
   The death of Lord Nelson: authentic narrative with the
   circumstances preceding, attending, and subsequent to, that
   event: the professional report of his lordship's wound and
   several interesting anecdotes.
   1. Nelson, Horatio Nelson, *Viscount*
   2. Great Britain, *Royal Navy*
   I. Title
   359.3'31'0924   DA87.1.N4

   ISBN 0–951037–00–5

The text of this fourth edition has been completely reset by
Photo-Graphics of Honiton, Devon
Printed and bound in Great Britain by A. Wheaton & Co
Ltd, Exeter

THE Surgeon of the late illustrious Lord NEL-SON feels himself called upon, from the responsible situation which he held on the eventful day of the 21st of October 1805, to lay before the British Nation the following Narrative. It contains an account of the most interesting incidents which occurred on board the Victory (Lord NELSON'S flag-ship) from the time of her sailing from England, in the month of September, till the day of battle inclusively; with a detail of the particulars of HIS LORDSHIP'S Death, the mode adopted for preserving his revered Remains during the subsequent long passage of the Victory to England, and the condition of the Body when it was deposited in Greenwich Hospital. This short statement of facts is deemed a small but necessary tribute of respect to the memory of the departed Hero, as well as a professional document which the Public had a right to expect from the man who had the melancholy honour of being his principal medical attendant on that occasion.

FOREWORD

EVERY YEAR in Wardroom Messes
the world, officers of the Royal Nav
Trafalgar Night dinner and drink a
the "Immortal Memory" of A
Nelson.

Thousands of speeches have been
extolling the qualities of Nelson as a
and as an Admiral and leader of me

His resolution, courage, tactical ski
leadership were legendary; his officer
men loved him. After the Battle of Tra
in a letter home one of his sailors wrot
the men in our ship who have seen hir
such soft toads they have done nothing
Blast their eyes and cry ever since he
killed".

What manner of man was it who insp
such trust in his "people" and whose ex
ple is revered by succeeding generation
Naval Officers?

In this dramatic account of his last gr
action we are privileged to have a first ha
account of "the Nelson Touch".

Liphook, Hampshire   C.A.W. WESTC
April 1985   REAR-ADMIR

Narrative

LORD NELSON sailed from St. Helen's in the Victory, with the Euryalus frigate, on the morning of the 15th of September 1805, to take the command of the British Fleet cruizing before Cadiz. On the 18th he appeared off Plymouth; where he was joined by his Majesty's ships Thunderer and Ajax, with which he proceeded for his destined station. On the 20th he communicated by private signal with the squadron under the command of Rear-Admiral STIRLING, which passed within a few miles of the Victory; and the same day at noon, spoke his Majesty's ship Le Decade, having on board Rear-Admiral Sir RICHARD BICK-

ERTON, who was on his return to England for the recovery of his health.

SOME bad weather and adverse winds were experienced by the Victory in crossing the Bay of Biscay, and on the 27th Cape St. Vincent was seen. Lord NELSON had dispatched the Euryalus ahead on the preceding day, to acquaint Admiral COLLINGWOOD with his approach; and to direct that no salute should take place, nor any public compliments be paid to his flag, on his assuming the command, as he wished the Enemy to be kept ignorant of a reinforcement being received by the British Fleet. In the evening of the 28th, the Victory joined the Fleet; now consisting of twenty-seven ships of the line, including the Victory, Ajax, and Thunderer: the city of Cadiz was seen distant about fifteen miles, with the Combined Fleets at anchor; and Admiral LOUIS, with five or six ships under his command, close in shore, watching the motions of the Enemy.

ON the 29th, prompt and decisive measures were adopted to prevent the Enemy from receiving any supplies of provisions by

sea, which HIS LORDSHIP was informed they
were very much distressed for: cruizers
were stationed off the Capes St. Vincent, St.
Mary's, and Trafalgar; and the frigates
Euryalus and Hydra were ordered to keep
off the entrance of Cadiz. HIS LORDSHIP
now retired with the Fleet to the vicinity of
Cape St. Mary's, about fifty or sixty miles
westward of Cadiz; keeping up a constant
communication with the frigates in shore,
by means of three or four ships of the line
placed at convenient intervals for disting-
uishing the signals of each other. This
distance from the Enemy's port was pre-
served by HIS LORDSHIP, to prevent them
from being speedily acquainted with the
force of the Fleet under his command; and
that he might avoid the necessity of bearing
up in bad weather, and running with the
Fleet through the Straits of Gibraltar when
the westerly gales prevailed: as the incon-
venience of being forced into the Mediterra-
nean, had been felt by former Commanders
in Chief; and would now have afforded a
favourable opportunity to the Enemy of
effecting their escape from Cadiz, or at all

events have rendered their obtaining supplies less difficult.

ON the 1st of October Admiral LOUIS joined the Fleet, with a part of his squadron (the Canopus, Spencer, and Tigre), from before Cadiz; and departed the next day with those ships, the Queen, and the Zealous, for Gibraltar, to procure a supply of provisions, stores, and water, which they were much in want of. On the 4th he rejoined with his squadron; having received intelligence from the Euryalus by telegraph, that the French ships in Cadiz were embarking their troops, and preparing to sail. Lord NELSON however conceived this to be merely intended as a stratagem to draw him nearer to Cadiz, for the purpose of obtaining a knowledge of his force; and therefore directed Admiral LOUIS to proceed in the execution of the orders before delivered to him.

BETWEEN the 7th and the 13th, HIS LORDSHIP was reinforced by the Royal Sovereign, Bellisle, Defiance, Agamemnon, and Africa, from England, and the Leviathan from Gibraltar. The Agamemnon, Sir EDWARD BERRY, joined on the 13th;[1] with intelligence that she had been chased on the coast of Portugal a few days before by an Enemy's squadron, consisting of six sail of the line.

ON the 13th in the evening, Sir ROBERT CALDER, in his Majesty's ship the Prince of Wales, parted company with the Fleet, on his return to England. His departure Lord NELSON had some days before evinced an anxious wish to procrastinate, and was heard that very day to declare his firm belief that the Combined Fleets would be at sea in the course of ten days or a fortnight.[2]

[1] BY THIS SHIP HIS LORDSHIP received some newspapers from England, one of which contained a paragraph stating that General MACK was about to be appointed to the command of the Austrian armies in Germany. On reading this, HIS LORDSHIP made the following observation: "I know General MACK too well. He sold the King of Naples; and if he is now entrusted with an important command, he will certainly betray the Austrian monarchy."

[2] CAPTAIN HARDY left England in a bad state of health, with which he had been afflicted during the last twelve months; but was now in a progressive state of amendment. Lord NELSON asked the Surgeon this day, "how long he thought it might be before Captain HARDY's perfect recovery;" and on the Surgeon's answering that "he hoped not more than a fortnight,"—"Ah!" replied HIS LORDSHIP, "before a fortnight the Enemy will be at sea, the business will be done, and we shall be looking out for England."

On the 18th the Donegal, Captain Mal-colm, left the Fleet for Gibraltar. On the 19th his Majesty's ships the Colossus, Mars, Defence, and Agamemnon, formed the cordon of communication with the frigates in shore: the Fleet was lying to. About half past nine in the morning, the Mars, being one of the ships nearest to the Fleet, repeated the signal from the ships further in shore, that "the Enemy were coming out of port." Lord Nelson immediately ordered the general signal to be made, with two guns, for a chace in the south-east quarter. The wind was now very light; and the breezes partial, mostly from the south-south-west. The Fleet made all possible sail; and about two o'clock the Colossus and Mars repeated signals from the ships in shore, communicating the welcome intelligence of "the Enemy being at sea." This cheered the minds of all on board, with the prospect of realizing those hopes of meeting the Enemy which had been so long and so sanguinely entertained. It was well known to His Lordship, that all the Enemy's ships had the iron hoops on their masts painted black; whereas the British ships, with the exception of the Bellisle and Polyphemus, had theirs painted yellow: and as he considered that this would serve for a very good mark of distinction in the heat of battle, he made known this circumstance to the Fleet, and ordered the Bellisle and Polyphemus to paint their hoops yellow; but the evening being far advanced when the signal was made to them for this purpose, His Lordship, fearing that it might not be distinctly understood, sent the Entreprenante cutter to them to communicate the order.

During the night the Fleet continued steering to the south-east under all sail, in expectation of seeing the Enemy; and at day-break on the 20th found itself in the entrance of the Straits of Gibraltar, but nothing of the Enemy to be discovered. The Fleet now wore, and made sail to the north-west; and at seven in the morning the Phœbe was seen making signals for "the Enemy bearing north." At eight o'clock the Victory hove to; and Admiral Collingwood, with the Captains of the Mars, Colossus, and Defence, came on board, to receive instructions from HIS LORDSHIP: at eleven minutes past nine they returned to their respective ships, and the Fleet made sail again to the northward.

IN the afternoon the wind increased, and blew fresh from the south-west; which excited much apprehension on board the Victory, lest the Enemy might be forced to return to port. The look-out ships, however, made several signals for seeing them, and to report their force and bearings. HIS LORDSHIP was at this time on the poop; and turning round, and observing a group of Midshipmen assembled together, he said to them with a smile, "This day or to-morrow will be a fortunate one for you, young men," alluding to their being promoted in the event of a victory.

A LITTLE before sunset the Euryalus communicated intelligence by telegraph, that "the Enemy appeared determined to go to the westward." HIS LORDSHIP upon this ordered it to be signified to Captain BLACK-WOOD (of that ship) by signal, that "he depended on the Euryalus for keeping sight

15

of the Enemy during the night." The night signals were so clearly and distinctly arranged by His Lordship, and so well understood by the respective Captains, that the Enemy's motions continued to be made known to him with the greatest facility throughout the night: a certain number of guns, with false fires and blue lights, announced their altering their course, wearing, and making or shortening sail; and signals communicating such changes were repeated by the look-out ships, from the Euryalus to the Victory.

The Enemy wore twice during the night: which evolution was considered by His Lordship as shewing an intention, on their part, of keeping the port of Cadiz open; and made him apprehend that on seeing the British Fleet, they would effect their retreat thither before he could bring them to a general action. He was therefore very careful not to approach their Fleet near enough to be seen by them before morning.

The British Fleet wore about two o'clock in the morning; and stood on the larboard tack with their heads to the northward, carrying their topsails and foresails, and anxiously expecting the dawn of day. When that period arrived, the Combined Fleets were distinctly seen from the Victory's deck, formed in a close line of battle ahead on the starboard tack, standing to the south, and about twelve miles to leeward. They consisted of thirty-three ships of the line; four of which were three-deckers, and one of seventy guns: the strength of the British Fleet was twenty-seven ships of the line; seven of which were three-deckers, and three of sixty-four guns. Lord NELSON had, on the 10th, issued written Instructions to the Admirals and Captains of the Fleet individually, pointing out his intended mode of attack in the event of meeting the Enemy;[3] and now, previously to appearing himself on deck, he directed Captain HARDY to make the necessary signals for the order and disposition of the Fleet accordingly.

HIS LORDSHIP came upon deck soon after day-light. he was dressed as usual in his

[3] THESE Instructions will be found at the end of the Narrative.

Admiral's frock-coat, bearing on the left breast four stars of different orders which he always wore with his common apparel.[4] He displayed excellent spirits, and expressed his pleasure at the prospect of giving a fatal blow to the naval power of France and Spain; and spoke with confidence of obtaining a signal victory notwithstanding the inferiority of the British Fleet, declaring to Captain HARDY that "he would not be contented with capturing less than twenty sail of the line." He afterwards pleasantly observed that "the 21st of October was the happiest day in the year among his family," but did not assign the reason of this.[5] HIS

[4] HIS LORDSHIP did not wear his sword in the Battle of Trafalgar: it had been taken from the place where it hung up in his cabin, and was laid ready on his table; but it is supposed he forgot to call for it. This was the only action in which he ever appeared without a sword.

[5] IT has been since recollected that on the 21st of October 1757, HIS LORDSHIP's maternal uncle, Captain SUCKLING, in the Dreadnought, in company with two other line of battle ships, attacked and beat off a French squadron of four sail of the line and three frigates, off Cape François. The French Commodore was towed into Cape François; and the English ships, being too much disabled to follow up their success, bore away to Jamaica to refit.

LORDSHIP had previously entertained a strong presentiment that this would prove the auspicious day; and had several times said to Captain HARDY and Doctor SCOTT (Chaplain of the ship, and Foreign Secretary to the Commander in Chief, whose intimate friendship he enjoyed), "The 21st of October will be our day."

THE wind was now from the west; but the breezes were very light, with a long heavy swell running. The signal being made for bearing down upon the Enemy in two lines, the British Fleet set all possible sail. The lee line, consisting of thirteen ships, was led by Admiral COLLINGWOOD in the Royal Sovereign; and the weather line, composed of fourteen ships, by the Commander in Chief in the Victory. His LORDSHIP had ascended the poop, to have a better view of both lines of the British Fleet; and while there, gave particular directions for taking down from his cabin the different fixtures, and for being very careful in removing the portrait of Lady HAMILTON: "Take care of my Guardian Angel," said he, addressing himself to the persons to be employed in this business. Immediately after this he quitted the poop, and retired to his cabin for a few minutes: where he committed to paper the following short but devout and fervent ejaculation, which must be universally admired as truly characteristic of the Christian hero; and the codicil to his will, which follows it:

"MAY the great GOD whom I worship, grant to my Country, and for the benefit of Europe in general, a great and glorious victory; and may no misconduct in any one tarnish it, and may humanity after victory be the predominant feature in the British Fleet! For myself individually, I commit my life to Him that made me; and may His blessing alight on my endeavours for serving my Country faithfully! To Him I resign myself, and the just cause which is entrusted to me to defend. Amen, Amen, Amen."   *   *   *

"OCTOBER 21st, 1805. *Then in sight of the Combined Fleets of France and Spain, distant about ten miles.*

"WHEREAS the eminent services of EMMA HAMILTON, widow of the Right

Honourable Sir WILLIAM HAMILTON, have been of the very greatest service to my King and Country, to my knowledge, without ever receiving any reward from either our King or Country:

FIRST, that she obtained the King of Spain's letter in 1796, to his brother the King of Naples, acquainting him of his intention to declare war against England; from which letter the ministry sent out orders to the then Sir JOHN JERVIS, to strike a stroke if opportunity offered, against either the arsenals of Spain or her fleets:—that neither of these was done, is not the fault of Lady HAMILTON; the opportunity might have been offered:[6]

"SECONDLY: the British Fleet under my command could never have returned the second time to Egypt, had not Lady HAMILTON's influence with the Queen of Naples caused letters to be wrote to the Governor of Syracuse, that he was to

[6] THIS phrase has been subjected to misconstruction; to the Writer of these pages, however, both the purport and expression of it seem very clear, thus: "*might have been offered*" (though it *was not*).

encourage the Fleet's being supplied with every thing, should they put into any port in Sicily. We put into Syracuse, and received every supply; went to Egypt, and destroyed the French Fleet:

"COULD I have rewarded these services, I would not now call upon my Country; but as that has not been in my power, I leave EMMA Lady HAMILTON therefore a legacy to my King and Country, that they will give her an ample provision to maintain her rank in life.

"I ALSO leave to the beneficence of my Country my adopted Daughter, HORATIA NELSON THOMPSON; and I desire she will use in future the name of NELSON only.

"THESE ARE THE ONLY FAVOURS I ASK OF MY KING AND COUNTRY, AT THIS MOMENT WHEN I AM GOING TO FIGHT THEIR BATTLE. MAY GOD bless my King and Country, and all those I hold dear! My Relations it is needless to mention: they will of course be amply provided for.

"NELSON and BRONTE.

"Witness { HENRY BLACKWOOD.
T. M. HARDY."

THE prayer and codicil were both written with HIS LORDSHIP's own hand, within three hours before the commencement of the engagement.

As the Victory drew near to the Enemy, HIS LORDSHIP, accompanied by Captain HARDY, and the Captains of the four frigates (Euryalus, Naiad, Sirius, and Phœbe) who had been called on board by signal to receive instructions, visited the different decks of the ship. He addressed the crew at their several quarters, admonishing them against firing a single shot without being sure of their object; and expressed himself to the Officers highly satisfied with the arrangements made at their respective stations.

IT was now plainly perceived by all on board the Victory, that from the very compact line which the Enemy had formed, they were determined to make one great effort to recover in some measure their long-lost naval reputation. They wore in succession about twenty minutes past seven o'clock; and stood on the larboard tack, with their heads toward Cadiz. They kept a good deal of sail set; steering about two points from the wind, with top-sails shivering. Their van was particularly closed, having the Santissima Trinidada and the Bucentaur the ninth and tenth ships, the latter the flag-ship of Admiral VILLENEUVE: but as the Admirals of the Combined Fleets declined shewing their flags till the heat of the battle was over, the former of these ships was only distinguished from the rest by her having four decks; and Lord NELSON ordered the Victory to be steered for her bow.

SEVERAL Officers of the ship now communicated to each other their sentiments of anxiety for HIS LORDSHIP's personal safety, to which every other consideration seemed to give way. Indeed all were confident of gaining a glorious victory, but the apprehensions for HIS LORDSHIP were great and general; and the Surgeon made known to Doctor SCOTT his fears that HIS LORDSHIP would be made the object of the Enemy's marksmen, and his desire that he might be entreated by somebody to cover the stars on his coat with a handkerchief.

Doctor SCOTT and Mr. SCOTT (Public Secretary) both observed, however, that such a request would have no effect; as they knew HIS LORDSHIP's sentiments on the subject so well, that they were sure he would be highly displeased with whoever should take the liberty of recommending any change in his dress on this account: and when the Surgeon declared to Mr. SCOTT that he would avail himself of the opportunity of making his sick-report for the day,[7] to submit his sentiments to the Admiral, Mr.

[7] THE Victory's sick-report for this day numbered only ten convalescents, who all attended their respective quarters during the battle; and the whole Fleet was in a high state of health. Indeed the excellent health enjoyed by the crew of the Victory from December 1804 up to this period, is perhaps unprecedented: and is attributable solely to Captain HARDY's attention to their subordination, temperance, warm clothing, and cleanliness; together with the means daily adopted to obviate the effects of moisture, and to accomplish the thorough ventilation of every part of the ship.

THE Victory arrived at Spithead from the memorable and arduous chace of the Enemies' Fleets to Egypt and the West Indies, in August 1805: and notwithstanding the operation of the unfavourable circumstances of rapid change of climate, and the privation of refreshments experienced in that chace, as well as frequent increase of

SCOTT replied, "Take care, Doctor, what you are about; I would not be the man to mention such a matter to him." The Surgeon notwithstanding persisted in his design, and remained on deck to find a proper opportunity for addressing HIS LORDSHIP; but this never occurred: as HIS LORDSHIP continued occupied with the Captain of the frigates (to whom he was explaining his intentions respecting the services they were to perform during the battle) till a short time before the Enemy opened their fire on the Royal Sovereign, when Lord NELSON ordered all persons not stationed on the quarter-deck or poop to repair to their proper quarters; and the Surgeon, much concerned at this dis-

---

numbers (as in the West Indies there were at one time embarked in her above 990 souls), there was not now a single hospital-patient on board, nor did any occur during the several weeks of her stay in England; with which Lord NELSON expressed himself highly pleased when he joined the ship again, on the 14th of September, at St. Helen's. The Victory's casualties from the 29th of December 1804 to the 20th of October following, were only five fatal cases (one of these by accidental injury), and two patients sent to a naval hospital.

appointment, retired from the deck with several other Officers.[8]

THE boats on the quarters of the ship, being found in the way of the guns, were now lowered down, and towed astern. Captain BLACKWOOD, of the Euryalus, remained on board the Victory till a few minutes before the Enemy began to fire upon her. He represented to HIS LORDSHIP, that his flag-ship would be singled out and much pressed by the Enemy; and suggested the propriety therefore of permitting one or two ships of his line to go ahead of the Victory, and lead her into action, which might be the means of drawing in some measure the Enemy's attention from her. To this Lord NELSON assented, and at half past nine o'clock he ordered the Temeraire and Leviathan by signal (the former of which ships, being close to the Victory, was hailed by HIS LORDSHIP) to go ahead for that purpose; but from the light breeze that prevailed they were unable, notwithstand-

[8] IT has been reported, but erroneously, that HIS LORDSHIP was actually requested by his Officers to change his dress, or to cover his stars.

ing their utmost efforts, to attain their intended stations. Captain BLACKWOOD foresaw that this would be the case; and as the Victory still continued to carry all her sail, he wished Captain HARDY to acquaint HIS LORDSHIP, that unless her sail was in some degree shortened, the two ships just mentioned could not succeed in getting ahead previously to the Enemy's line being forced: this however Captain HARDY declined doing, as he conceived HIS LORDSHIP's ardour to get into battle would on no account suffer such a measure.[9]

ABOUT half an hour before the Enemy opened their fire, the memorable telegraphic signal was made, that "ENGLAND EXPECTS EVERY MAN WILL DO HIS DUTY," which was spread and received throughout the Fleet with enthusiasm. It is impossible adequately to describe by any language, the lively emotions excited in the crew of the

[9] HIS LORDSHIP just at this time found fault with the Officer commanding on the forecastle, because the lee (or starboard) lower studding-sail had not been set sooner; a circumstance which, though trivial in itself, shews how well Captain HARDY knew HIS LORDSHIP's sentiments.

Victory when this propitious communication was made known to them: confidence and resolution were strongly pourtrayed in the countenance of all; and the sentiment generally expressed to each other was, that they would prove to their Country that day, how well British seamen *could* "do their duty" when led to battle by their revered Admiral. The signal was afterwards made to "prepare to anchor after the close of the day;" and union-jacks were hoisted at the fore-top-mast and top-gallant-stays of each ship, to serve as a distinction from the Enemy's, in conformity with orders previously issued by the Commander in Chief. By His LORDSHIP's directions also, the different divisions of the Fleet hoisted the St. George's or white ensign, being the colours of the Commander in Chief: this was done to prevent confusion from occurring during the battle, through a variety of national flags.

THE Royal Sovereign now made the signal by telegraph, that "the Enemy's Commander in Chief was in a frigate." This mistake arose from one of their frigates making many signals. Lord NELSON ordered his line to be steered about two points more to the northward than that of his Second in Command, for the purpose of cutting off the retreat of the Enemy's van to the port of Cadiz; which was the reason of the three leading ships of Admiral COLLING-WOOD's line being engaged with the Enemy previously to those of the Commander in Chief's line.

THE Enemy began to fire on the Royal Sovereign at thirty minutes past eleven o'clock; in ten minutes after which she got under the stern of the St. Anna, and commenced a fire on her. Lieutenant PASCO, Signal Officer of the Victory, was heard to say while looking through his glass, "There is a top-gallant-yard gone." HIS LORDSHIP eagerly asked, "Whose top-gallant-yard is that gone? Is it the Royal Sovereign's?" and on being answered by Lieutenant PASCO in the negative, and that it was the Enemy's, he smiled, and said: "COLLINGWOOD is doing well."[1]

---

[1] HIS LORDSHIP in a few minutes after this called Lieutenant PASCO, Mr. OGILVIE, and some other Officers, near him, and desired them to set their watches by the time of that which HIS LORDSHIP wore.

AT fifty minutes past eleven the Enemy opened their fire on the Commander in Chief. They shewed great coolness in the commencement of the battle; for as the Victory approached their line, their ships lying immediately ahead of her and across her bows fired only one gun at a time, to ascertain whether she was yet within their range. This was frequently repeated by eight or nine of their ships, till at length a shot passed through the Victory's main-top-gallant-sail; the hole in which being discovered by the Enemy, they immediately opened their broadsides, supporting an awful and tremendous fire. In a very short time afterwards, Mr. SCOTT, Public Secretary to the Commander in Chief, was killed by a cannon-shot while in conversation with Captain HARDY. Lord NELSON being then near them, Captain ADAIR of the Marines, with the assistance of a Seaman, endeavoured to remove the body from HIS LORDSHIP'S sight: but he had already observed the fall of his Secretary; and now said with anxiety, "Is that poor SCOTT that is gone?" and on being answered in the affirmative by Captain ADAIR, he replied, "Poor fellow!"

Lord NELSON and Captain HARDY walked the quarter-deck in conversation for some time after this, while the Enemy kept up an incessant raking fire. A double-headed shot struck one of the parties of Marines drawn up on the poop, and killed eight of them; when HIS LORDSHIP, perceiving this, ordered Captain ADAIR to disperse his men round the ship, that they might not suffer so much from being together. In a few minutes afterwards a shot struck the fore-brace-bits on the quarter-deck, and passed between Lord NELSON and Captain HARDY; a splinter from the bits bruising Captain HARDY's foot, and tearing the buckle from his shoe. They both instantly stopped; and were observed by the Officers on deck to survey each other with inquiring looks, each supposing the other to be wounded. HIS LORDSHIP then smiled, and said: "This is too warm work, HARDY, to last long;" and declared that "through all the battles he had been in, he had never witnessed more cool courage than was displayed by the Victory's crew on this occasion."

THE Victory by this time, having approached close to the Enemy's van, had suffered very severely without firing a single gun: she had lost about twenty men killed, and had about thirty wounded. Her mizen-topmast, and all her studding-sails and their booms, on both sides were shot away; the Enemy's fire being chiefly directed at her rigging, with a view to disable her before she could close with them.[2] At four minutes past twelve o'clock she opened her fire, from both sides of her decks, upon the Enemy; when Captain HARDY represented to HIS LORDSHIP, that "it appeared impracticable to pass through the Enemy's line without going on board some one of their ships." Lord NELSON answered, "I cannot help it: it does not signify which we run on

---

[2] THE Enemy's fire continued to be pointed so high throughout the engagement, that the Victory did not lose a man on her lower deck; and had only two wounded on that deck; and these by musket-balls.

board of; go on board which you please; take your choice."

At twenty minutes past twelve, the tiller-ropes being shot away, Mr. Atkinson, the Master, was ordered below to get the helm put to port; which being done, the Victory was soon run on board the Redoutable of seventy-four guns. On coming alongside and nearly on board of her, that ship fired her broadside into the Victory, and immediately let down her lower-deck ports; which, as has been since learnt, was done to prevent her from being boarded through them by the Victory's crew. She never fired a great gun after this single broadside. A few minutes after this, the Temeraire fell likewise on board of the Redoutable, on the side opposite to the Victory; having also an Enemy's ship, said to be La Fougueux, on board of *her* on her other side: so that the extraordinary and unprecedented circumstance occurred here, of *four* ships of the line being *on board of each other* in the heat of battle; forming as compact a tier as if they had been moored together, their heads lying all the same way. The Temeraire, as

DLN–C

was just before mentioned, was between the Redoutable and La Fougueux. The Redoutable commenced a heavy fire of musketry from the tops, which was continued for a considerable time with destructive effect to the Victory's crew: her great guns however being silent, it was supposed at different times that she had surrendered; and in consequence of this opinion, the Victory twice ceased firing upon her, by orders transmitted from the quarter-deck.

AT this period, scarcely a person in the Victory escaped unhurt who was exposed to the Enemy's musketry; but there were frequent huzzas and cheers heard from between the decks, in token of the surrender of different of the Enemy's ships. An incessant fire was kept up from both sides of the Victory: her larboard guns played upon the Santissima Trinidada and the Bucentaur; and the starboard guns of the middle and lower decks were depressed, and fired with a diminished charge of powder, and three shot each, into the Redoutable. This mode of firing was adopted by Lieutenants WIL-LIAMS, KING, YULE, and BROWN, to obviate

the danger of the Temeraire's suffering
from the Victory's shot passing through the
Redoutable; which must have been the case
if the usual quantity of powder, and the
common elevation, had been given to the
guns.—A circumstance occurred in this
situation, which shewed in a most striking
manner the cool intrepidity of the Officers
and men stationed on the lower deck of the
Victory. When the guns on this deck were
run out, their muzzles came into contact
with the Redoutable's side; and consequently at every discharge there was reason
to fear that the Enemy would take fire, and
both the Victory and the Temeraire be
involved in her flames. Here then was seen
the astonishing spectacle of the fireman of
each gun standing ready with a bucket full
of water, which as soon as his gun was
discharged he dashed into the Enemy
through the holes made in her side by the
shot.

IT was from this ship (the Redoutable)
that Lord NELSON received his mortal
wound. About fifteen minutes past one
o'clock, which was in the heat of the en-

gagement, he was walking the middle of the quarter-deck with Captain HARDY, and in the act of turning near the hatchway with his face towards the stern of the Victory, when the fatal ball was fired from the Enemy's mizen-top; which, from the situation of the two ships (lying on board of each other), was brought just abaft, and rather below, the Victory's main-yard, and of course not more than fifteen yards distant from that part of the deck where HIS LORDSHIP stood. The ball struck the epaulette on his left shoulder, and penetrated his chest. He fell with his face on the deck. Captain HARDY, who was on his right (the side furthest from the Enemy) and advanced some steps before HIS LORDSHIP, on turning round, saw the Serjeant Major (SECKER) of Marines with two Seamen raising him from the deck; where he had fallen on the same spot on which, a little before, his Secretary had breathed his last, with whose blood HIS LORDSHIP's clothes were much soiled. Captain HARDY expressed a hope that he was not severely wounded; to which the gallant Chief replied: "They have done for me at last, HARDY." — "I hope not," answered Captain HARDY. "Yes." replied HIS LORDSHIP; "my backbone is shot through."

CAPTAIN HARDY ordered the Seamen to carry the Admiral to the cockpit; and now two incidents occurred strikingly characteristic of this great man, and strongly marking that energy and reflection which in his heroic mind rose superior even to the immediate consideration of his present awful condition. While the men were carrying him down the ladder from the middle deck, HIS LORDSHIP observed that the tiller-ropes were not yet replaced; and desired one of the Midshipmen stationed there to go upon the quarter-deck and remind Captain HARDY of that circumstance, and request that new ones should be immediately rove. Having delivered this order, he took his handkerchief from his pocket and covered his face with it, that he might be conveyed to the cockpit at this crisis unnoticed by the crew.

SEVERAL wounded Officers, and about forty men, were likewise carried to the

Surgeon for assistance just at this time; and some others had breathed their last during their conveyance below. Among the latter were Lieutenant WILLIAM ANDREW RAM, and Mr. WHIPPLE Captain's Clerk. The Surgeon had just examined these two Officers, and found that they were dead,[3] when his attention was arrested by several of the wounded calling to him, "Mr. BEAT-TY, Lord NELSON is here: Mr. BEATTY, the Admiral is wounded." The Surgeon now, on looking round, saw the handkerchief fall from HIS LORDSHIP's face; when the stars on his coat, which also had been covered by it, appeared. Mr. BURKE the Purser, and the Surgeon, ran immediately to the assistance of HIS LORDSHIP, and took him from the arms of the Seamen who had carried him below. In conveying him to one of the Midshipmen's births, they stumbled, but recovered themselves without falling. Lord NELSON then inquired who were supporting him; and when the Surgeon informed him,

---

[3] THE reader may judge of the Surgeon's feelings at this momentous period, when informed that that excellent young Officer Mr. RAM was one of his dearest friends.

HIS LORDSHIP replied, "Ah, Mr. BEATTY! you can do nothing for me. I have but a short time to live: my back is shot through." The Surgeon said, "he hoped the wound was not so dangerous as HIS LORDSHIP imagined, and that he might still survive long to enjoy his glorious victory." The Reverend Doctor SCOTT, who had been absent in another part of the cockpit administering lemonade to the wounded, now came instantly to HIS LORDSHIP; and in the anguish of grief wrung his hands, and said: "Alas, BEATTY, how prophetic you were!" alluding to the apprehensions expressed by the Surgeon for HIS LORDSHIP's safety previous to the battle.

HIS LORDSHIP was laid upon a bed, stripped of his clothes, and covered with a sheet. While this was effecting, he said to Doctor SCOTT, "Doctor, I told you so. Doctor, I am gone;" and after a short pause he added in a low voice, "I have to leave Lady HAMILTON, and my adopted daughter HORATIA, as a legacy to my Country." The Surgeon then examined the wound, assuring HIS LORDSHIP that he would not put him to much pain in endeavouring to discover the course of the ball; which he soon found had penetrated deep into the chest, and had probably lodged in the spine. This being explained to HIS LORDSHIP, he replied, "he was confident his back was shot through." The back was then examined externally, but without any injury being perceived; on which HIS LORDSHIP was requested by the Surgeon to make him acquainted with all his sensations. He replied, that "he felt a gush of blood every minute within his breast: that he had no feeling in the lower part of his body: and that his breathing was difficult, and attended with very severe pain about that part of the spine where he was confident that the ball had struck; for," said he, "I felt it break my back." These symptoms, but more particularly the gush of blood which HIS LORDSHIP complained of, together with the state of his pulse, indicated to the Surgeon the hopeless situation of the case; but till after the victory was ascertained and announced to HIS LORDSHIP, the true nature of his wound was concealed by the Surgeon from all on board except only Captain HARDY, Doctor SCOTT, Mr. BURKE, and Messrs. SMITH and WESTEMBURG the Assistant Surgeons.

THE Victory's crew cheered whenever they observed an Enemy's ship surrender. On one of these occasions, Lord NELSON anxiously inquired what was the cause of it; when Lieutenant PASCO, who lay wounded at some distance from HIS LORDSHIP, raised himself up, and told him that another ship had struck, which appeared to give him much satisfaction. He now felt an ardent thirst; and frequently called for drink, and to be fanned with paper, making use of these words: "Fan, fan," and "Drink, drink." This he continued to repeat, when he wished for drink or the refreshment of cool air, till a very few minutes before he expired. Lemonade, and wine and water, were given to him occasionally. He evinced great solicitude for the event of the battle, and fears for the safety of his friend Captain HARDY. Doctor SCOTT and Mr. BURKE used every argument they could suggest, to relieve his anxiety. Mr. BURKE told him "the Enemy were decisively defeated, and that he hoped His Lordship would still live to be himself the bearer of the joyful tidings to his country." He replied, "It is nonsense, Mr. Burke, to suppose I can live: my sufferings are great, but they will all be soon over." Doctor Scott entreated His Lordship "not to despair of living," and said "he trusted that Divine Providence would restore him once more to his dear Country and friends."—"Ah, Doctor!" replied His Lordship, "it is all over; it is all over."

Many messages were sent to Captain Hardy by the Surgeon, requesting his attendance on His Lordship; who became impatient to see him, and often exclaimed: "Will no one bring Hardy to me? He must be killed: he is surely destroyed." The Captain's Aide-de-camp, Mr. Bulkley, now came below, and stated that "circumstances respecting the Fleet required Captain Hardy's presence on deck, but that he would avail himself of the first favourable moment to visit His Lordship" On hearing him deliver this message to the Surgeon, His Lordship inquired who had brought it.

Mr. BURKE answered, "It is Mr. BULKLEY, my Lord." —"It is his voice," replied HIS LORDSHIP: he then said to the young gentleman, "Remember me to your father."

AN hour and ten minutes however elapsed, from the time of HIS LORDSHIP'S being wounded, before Captain HARDY'S first subsequent interview with him; the particulars of which are nearly as follow. They shook hands affectionately, and Lord NELSON said: "Well, HARDY, how goes the battle? How goes the day with us?"—"Very well, my Lord," replied Captain HARDY: "we have got twelve or fourteen of the Enemy's ships in our possession; but five of their van have tacked, and shew an intention of bearing down upon the Victory. I have therefore called two or three of our fresh ships round us, and have no doubt of giving them a drubbing."—"I hope," said HIS LORDSHIP, "none of *our* ships have struck, HARDY."—"No, my Lord," replied Captain HARDY; "there is no fear of that." Lord NELSON then said: "I am a dead man, HARDY. I am going fast: it will be all over with me soon. Come nearer to me. Pray let my dear Lady HAMILTON have my hair, and all other things belonging to me." Mr. BURKE was about to withdraw at the commencement of this conversation; but HIS LORDSHIP, perceiving his intention, desired he would remain. Captain HARDY observed, that "he hoped Mr. BEATTY could yet hold out some prospect of life."—"Oh! no," answered HIS LORDSHIP; "it is impossible. My back is shot through. BEATTY will tell you so." Captain HARDY then returned on deck, and at parting shook hands again with his revered friend and commander.

HIS LORDSHIP now requested the Surgeon, who had been previously absent a short time attending Mr. RIVERS, to return to the wounded, and give his assistance to such of them as he could be useful to; "for," said he, "you can do nothing for me." The Surgeon assured him that the Assistant Surgeons were doing every thing that could be effected for those unfortunate men; but on HIS LORDSHIP's several times repeating his injunctions to that purpose, he left him surrounded by Doctor SCOTT, Mr. BURKE,

and two of His LORDSHIP's domestics. After
the Surgeon had been absent a few minutes
attending Lieutenants PEAKE and REEVES
of the Marines, who were wounded, he was
called by Doctor SCOTT to HIS LORDSHIP,
who said: "Ah, Mr. BEATTY! I have sent for
you to say, what I forgot to tell you before,
that all power of motion and feeling below
my breast are gone; and *you*," continued he,
"very well *know* I can live but a short time."
The emphatic manner in which he pronounced these last words, left no doubt in
the Surgeon's mind, that he adverted to the
case of a man who had some months before
received a mortal injury of the spine on
board the Victory, and had laboured under
similar privations of sense and muscular
motion. The case had made a great impression on Lord NELSON: he was anxious
to know the cause of such symptoms, which
was accordingly explained to him; and he
now appeared to apply the situation and
fate of this man to himself.[4] The Surgeon

---

[4] THE instance here alluded to occurred in the month of
July, in the Victory's return to Europe from the West
Indies; and the man survived the injury thirteen days.

answered, "My Lord, you told me so before:" but he now examined the extremities, to ascertain the fact; when HIS LORDSHIP said, "Ah, BEATTY! I am too certain of it: SCOTT and BURKE have tried it already. You *know* I am gone." The Surgeon replied: "My Lord, unhappily for our Country, nothing can be done for you;" and having made this declaration he was so much affected, that he turned round and withdrew a few steps to conceal his emotions. HIS LORDSHIP said: "I know it. I feel something rising in my breast," putting his hand on his left side, "which tells me I am gone." Drink was recommended liberally, and Doctor SCOTT and Mr. BURKE fanned him with paper. He often exclaimed, "GOD be praised, I have done my duty;" and upon the Surgeon's inquiring whether his pain was still very great, he declared, "it continued so very severe, that he wished he was dead. Yet," said he in a lower voice, "one

His LORDSHIP, during the whole of that time, manifested much anxiety at the protracted sufferings of an individual whose dissolution was certain, and was expected every hour.

would like to live a little longer, too:" and
after a pause of a few minutes, he added in
the same tone, "What would become of
poor Lady HAMILTON, if she knew my situation!"

THE Surgeon, finding it impossible to
render HIS LORDSHIP any further assistance, left him, to attend Lieutenant BLIGH,
Messrs. SMITH and WESTPHALL Midshipmen, and some Seamen, recently wounded.
Captain HARDY now came to the cockpit to
see HIS LORDSHIP a second time, which was
after an interval of about fifty minutes from
the conclusion of his first visit. Before he
quitted the deck, he sent Lieutenant HILLS
to acquaint Admiral COLLINGWOOD with
the lamentable circumstance of Lord NEL-
SON's being wounded.[5]—Lord NELSON and

---

[5] CAPTAIN HARDY deemed it his duty to give this
information to Admiral COLLINGWOOD as soon as the fate
of the day was decided; but thinking that HIS LORDSHIP
might feel some repugnance to this communication, he
left directions for Lieutenant HILLS to be detained on
deck at his return, till he himself (Captain HARDY)
should come up from the cockpit. Lieutenant HILLS was
dispatched on this mission from the Victory, at the very
time when the Enemy's van ships that had tacked were
passing her to windward and firing at her.

Captain HARDY shook hands again: and while the Captain retained HIS LORDSHIP's hand, he congratulated him even in the arms of Death on his brilliant victory; "which," he said, "was complete; though he did not know how many of the Enemy were captured, as it was impossible to perceive every ship distinctly. He was certain however of fourteen or fifteen having surrendered." HIS LORDSHIP answered, "That is well, but I bargained for twenty:" and then emphatically exclaimed, *"Anchor, HARDY, anchor!"* To this the Captain replied: "I suppose, my Lord, Admiral COLLINGWOOD will now take upon himself the direction of affairs."—"Not while I live, I hope, HARDY!" cried the dying Chief; and at that moment endeavoured ineffectually to raise himself from the bed. "No," added he; "do *you* anchor, HARDY." Captain HARDY then said: "Shall *we* make the signal, Sir?"—"Yes," answered HIS LORDSHIP; "for if I live, I'll anchor."[6] The energetic man-

---

[6] MEANING that in case of HIS LORDSHIP's surviving till all resistance on the part of the Enemy had ceased, Captain HARDY was then to anchor the British Fleet and the prizes, if it should be found practicable.

ner in which he uttered these his last orders
to Captain HARDY, accompanied with his
efforts to raise himself, evinced his deter-
mination never to resign the command
while he retained the exercise of his trans-
cendant faculties, and that he expected
Captain HARDY still to carry into effect the
suggestions of his exalted mind; a sense of
his duty overcoming the pains of death. He
then told Captain HARDY, "he felt that in a
few minutes he should be no more;" adding
in a low tone, "Don't throw me overboard,
HARDY." The Captain answered: "Oh! no,
certainly not."—"Then," replied HIS
LORDSHIP, "you know what to do:[7] and,"
continued he, "take care of my dear Lady
HAMILTON, HARDY; take care of poor Lady
HAMILTON. Kiss me, HARDY." The Captain
now knelt down, and kissed his cheek; when
HIS LORDSHIP said, "Now I am satisfied.
Thank GOD, I have done my duty." Captain HARDY stood for a minute or two in
silent contemplation: he then knelt down

---

[7] ALLUDING to some wishes previously expressed by HIS
LORDSHIP to Captain HARDY respecting the place of his
interment.

again, and kissed HIS LORDSHIP's forehead. HIS LORDSHIP said: "Who is that?" The Captain answered: "It is HARDY;" to which HIS LORDSHIP replied, "GOD bless you, HARDY!" After this affecting scene Captain HARDY withdrew, and returned to the quarter-deck, having spent about eight minutes in this his last interview with his dying friend.

LORD NELSON now desired Mr. CHEVALIER, his Steward, to turn him upon his right side; which being effected, HIS LORDSHIP said: "I wish I had not left the deck, for I shall soon be gone." He afterwards became very low; his breathing was oppressed, and his voice faint. He said to Doctor SCOTT, "Doctor, I have *not* been a *great* sinner;" and after a short pause, "*Remember*, that I leave Lady HAMILTON and my Daughter HORATIA as a legacy to my Country: and," added he, "never forget HORATIA." His thirst now increased; and he called for "Drink, drink," "Fan, fan," and "Rub, rub:" addressing himself in the last case to Doctor SCOTT, who had been rubbing HIS LORDSHIP's breast with his hand,

from which he found some relief. These
words he spoke in a very rapid manner,
which rendered his articulation difficult:
but he every now and then, with evident
increase of pain, made a greater effort with
his vocal powers, and pronounced distinctly
these last words: "Thank GOD, I have done
my duty;" and this great sentiment he
continued to repeat as long as he was able
to give it utterance.

HIS LORDSHIP became speechless in about fifteen minutes after Captain HARDY
left him. Doctor SCOTT and Mr. BURKE,
who had all along sustained the bed under
his shoulders (which raised him in nearly a
semi-recumbent posture, the only one that
was supportable to him), forbore to disturb
him by speaking to him; and when he had
remained speechless about five minutes,
HIS LORDSHIP'S Steward went to the
Surgeon, who had been a short time occupied with the wounded in another part of
the cockpit, and stated his apprehensions
that HIS LORDSHIP was dying. The Surgeon
immediately repaired to him, and found
him on the verge of dissolution. He knelt

down by his side, and took up his hand; which was cold, and the pulse gone from the wrist. On the Surgeon's feeling his forehead, which was likewise cold, HIS LORDSHIP opened his eyes, looked up, and shut them again. The Surgeon again left him, and returned to the wounded who required his assistance; but was not absent five minutes before the Steward announced to him that "he believed HIS LORDSHIP had expired." The Surgeon returned, and found that the report was but too well founded: HIS LORDSHIP had breathed his last, at thirty minutes past four o'clock; at which period Doctor SCOTT was in the act of rubbing HIS LORDSHIP's breast, and Mr. BURKE supporting the bed under his shoulders.[8]

THUS died this matchless Hero, after performing, in a short but brilliant and well-

---

[8] IT must occur to the reader, that from the nature of the scene passing in the cockpit, and the noise of the guns, the whole of HIS LORDSHIP's expressions could not be borne in mind, nor even distinctly heard, by the different persons attending him. The most interesting parts are here detailed.

filled life, a series of naval exploits unexampled in any age of the world. None of the sons of Fame ever possessed greater zeal to promote the honour and interest of his King and Country; none ever served them with more devotedness and glory, or with more successful and important results. His character will for ever cast a lustre over the annals of this nation, to whose enemies his very name was a terror. In the battle off CAPE ST. VINCENT, though then in the subordinate station of a Captain, his unprecedented personal prowess will long be recorded with admiration among his profession. The shores of ABOUKIR and COPENHAGEN subsequently witnessed those stupendous achievements which struck the whole civilized world with astonishment. Still these were only preludes to the BATTLE OF TRAFALGAR: in which he shone with a majesty of dignity as far surpassing even his own former renown, as that renown had already exceeded every thing else to be found in the pages of naval history; the transcendantly brightest star in a galaxy of heroes. His splendid example will operate as an everlasting impulse to the enterprising genius of the British Navy.[9]

FROM the time of HIS LORDSHIP's being wounded till his death, a period of about two hours and forty-five minutes elapsed; but a knowledge of the decisive victory which was gained, he acquired of Captain HARDY within the first hour-and-a-quarter of this period. A partial canonade, however, was still maintained, in consequence of the Enemy's running ships passing the British at different points; and the last distant guns which were fired at their van ships that were making off, were heard a minute or two before HIS LORDSHIP expired.

A STEADY and continued fire was kept up by the Victory's starboard guns on the Redoutable, for about fifteen minutes after Lord NELSON was wounded; in which short period Captain ADAIR and about eighteen Seamen and Marines were killed, and Lieutenant BLIGH, Mr. PALMER Midship-

[9] IMMEDIATELY after HIS LORDSHIP expired, Captain HARDY went on board the Royal Sovereign, to communicate the melancholy event, and the nature of HIS LORDSHIP's last orders, to Admiral COLLINGWOOD.

man, and twenty Seamen and Marines, wounded, by the Enemy's musketry alone. The Redoutable had been on fire twice, in her fore-chains and on her forecastle: she had likewise succeeded in throwing a few hand-grenades into the Victory, which set fire to some ropes and canvas on the booms. The cry of "Fire!" was now circulated throughout the ship, and even reached the cockpit, without producing the degree of sensation which might be expected on such an awful occasion: the crew soon extinguished the fire on the booms, and then immediately turned their attention to that on board the Enemy; which they likewise put out by throwing buckets of water from the gangway into the Enemy's chains and forecastle, thus furnishing another admirable instance of deliberate intrepidity. At thirty minutes past one o'clock, the Redoutable's musketry having ceased, and her colours being struck, the Victory's men endeavoured to get on board her: but this was found impracticable; for though the two ships were still in contact, yet the top-sides or upper-works of both fell in so much on their upper decks, that there was a great space (perhaps fourteen feet or more) between their gangways; and the Enemy's ports being down, she could not be boarded from the Victory's lower nor middle deck. Several Seamen volunteered their services to Lieutenant QUILLIAM, to jump overboard, swim under the Redoutable's bows, and endeavour to get up there; but Captain HARDY refused to permit this. The prize however, and the Victory, fell off from each other; and their separation was believed to be the effect of the concussion produced by the Victory's fire, assisted by the helm of the latter being put to starboard.

MESSRS. OGILVIE and COLLINGWOOD, Midshipmen of the Victory, were sent in a small boat to take charge of the prize, which they effected.[1] After this, the ships of the Enemy's van that had shewn a disposition

---

[1] THE Redoutable lay alongside and still foul of the Temeraire for some time after this, and till several Seamen were sent from the latter to the assistance of the two Officers and men belonging to the Victory who had before taken possession of the prize.

to attack the Victory, passed to windward; and fired their broadsides not only into her and the Temeraire, but also into the French and Spanish captured ships indiscriminately: and they were seen to back or shiver their topsails for the purpose of doing this with more precision.[2] The two Midshipmen of the Victory had just boarded the Redoutable, and got their men out of the boat, when a shot from the Enemy's van ships that were making off cut the boat adrift. About ten minutes after taking possession of her, a Midshipman came to her from the Temeraire; and had hardly ascended the poop, when a shot from one of those ships took off his leg. The French Officers, seeing the firing continued on the prize by their own countrymen, entreated the English Midshipmen to quit the deck, and accompany them below. The unfortunate Mid-

2 THESE were the ships commanded by Admiral DUMAN-NOIR, and afterwards captured by the squadron under the command of Sir RICHARD STRACHAN. They were nearly half an hour in passing to windward, during the whole of which time they continued firing on the British ships.

shipman of the Temeraire was carried to
the French Surgeon, who was ordered to
give his immediate attendance to him in
preference to his own wounded: his leg was
amputated, but he died the same night. The
Redoutable suffered so much from shot
received between wind and water, that she
sunk while in tow of the Swiftsure on the
following evening, when the gale came on;
and out of a crew originally consisting of
more than eight hundred men, only about a
hundred and thirty were saved: but she had
lost above three hundred in the battle.[3]

IT is by no means certain, though highly
probable, that Lord NELSON was particularly aimed at by the Enemy. There were only
two Frenchmen left alive in the mizen-top
of the Redoutable at the time of HIS
LORDSHIP's being wounded, and by the
hands of one of these he fell. These men
continued firing at Captains HARDY and
ADAIR, Lieutenant ROTELY of the Marines,

[3] ABOUT twenty of the Redoutable's guns were dismounted in the action. Those on that side of her lower
deck opposed to the Victory, were all dismounted except
five or six.

and some of the Midshipmen on the Victory's poop, for some time afterwards. At length one of them was killed by a musket-ball: and on the other's then attempting to make his escape from the top down the rigging, Mr. POLLARD (Midshipman) fired his musket at him, and shot him in the back; when he fell dead from the shrouds, on the Redoutable's poop.

THE Writer of this will not attempt to depict the heart-rending sorrow, and melancholy gloom, which pervaded the breast and the countenance of every individual on board the Victory when HIS LORDSHIP's death became generally known. The anguish felt by all for such a loss, rendered doubly heavy to *them*, is more easy to be conceived than described: by his lamented fall they were at once deprived of their adored commander, and their friend and patron.

THE battle was fought in soundings about sixteen miles to the westward of Cape Trafalgar; and if fortunately there had been more wind in the beginning of the action, it is very probable that Lord NELSON would still have been saved to his Country, and that every ship of the line composing the Combined Fleets would have been either captured or destroyed: for had the Victory been going fast through the water, she must have dismasted the Redoutable, and would of course have passed on to attack another ship; consequently HIS LORDSHIP would not have been so long nor so much exposed to the Enemy's musketry. From the same circumstance of there being but little wind, several of the Enemy's ships made off before the rear and bad-sailing ships of the British lines could come up to secure them.

THE Victory had no musketry in her tops: as HIS LORDSHIP had a strong aversion to small arms being placed there, from the danger of their setting fire to the sails; which was exemplified by the destruction of the French ship L'Achille in this battle. It is a species of warfare by which individuals may suffer, and now and then a Commander be picked off: but it never can decide the fate of a general engagement; and a circumstance in many respects similar to that of the Victory's running on board of the

Redoutable, may not occur again in the course of centuries. The loss sustained by the Victory amounted to fifty-five killed, and a hundred and two wounded;[4] and it is highly honourable to the discipline and established regulations of the ship, that not one casualty from accident occurred on board during the engagement.

ON the day after the battle, as soon as circumstances permitted the Surgeon to devote a portion of his attention to the care of Lord NELSON's honoured Remains, measures were adopted to preserve them as effectually as the means then on board the Victory allowed. On the Surgeon's examining the nature of the wound, and the course of the ball, a quantity of blood was evacuated from the left side of the breast: none had escaped before. The ball was traced by a probe to the spine, but its lodgment could not at that time be discovered. There was

---

[4] MANY of those who were slightly wounded did not apply for assistance till after the public return of killed and wounded had been transmitted to Admiral COLLINGWOOD, which therefore reports a smaller number than here stated.

no lead on board to make a coffin: a cask called a leaguer, which is of the largest size on shipboard, was therefore chosen for the reception of the Body; which, after the hair had been cut off, was stripped of the clothes except the shirt, and put into it, and the cask was then filled with brandy.[5]

In the evening after this melancholy task was accomplished, the gale came on with violence from the south-west, and continued that night and the succeeding day without any abatement. During this boisterous weather, Lord NELSON's Body remained under the charge of a sentinel on the middle deck. The cask was placed on its

[5] BRANDY was recommended by the Surgeon in preference to rum, of which spirit also there was plenty on board. This circumstance is here noticed, because a very general but erroneous opinion was found to prevail on the Victory's arrival in England, that rum preserves the dead body from decay much longer and more perfectly than any other spirit, and ought therefore to have been used: but the fact is quite the reverse, for there are several kinds of spirit much better for that purpose than rum; and as their appropriateness in this respect arises from their degree of strength, on which alone their antiseptic quality depends, brandy is superior. Spirit of wine, however, is certainly by far the best, when it can be procured.

end, having a closed aperture at its top and another below; the object of which was, that as a frequent renewal of the spirit was thought necessary, the old could thus be drawn off below and a fresh quantity introduced above, without moving the cask, or occasioning the least agitation of the Body. On the 24th there was a disengagement of air from the Body to such a degree, that the sentinel became alarmed on seeing the head of the cask raised: he therefore applied to the Officers, who were under the necessity of having the cask spiled to give the air a discharge. After this, no considerable collection of air took place. The spirit was drawn off once, and the cask filled again, before the arrival of the Victory at Gibraltar (on the 28th of October): where spirit of wine was procured; and the cask, shewing a deficit produced by the Body's absorbing a considerable quantity of the brandy, was then filled up with it.

On the 29th the Victory's Seamen and Marines dangerously wounded in the action, were sent on shore to the naval hospital at Gibraltar. The interval between this

day and the 2nd of November was employed in repairing the damage sustained
by the ship, erecting jury-masts, fitting her
rigging, and completing her in every respect
for the voyage to England. On the 2nd of
November, preparations were made on
board to receive the wounded from the
hospital, who had unanimously entreated
Captain HARDY not to leave them behind:
but their embarkation could not be effected
this day; and the Victory being ordered to
quit the anchorage in Gibraltar Bay, to
make room for the disabled ships and prizes
daily arriving, she sailed in the evening for
Tetuan Bay, for the purpose of taking on
board a supply of fresh water, and awaiting
there a favourable wind to pass the Straits.
During the night however, and before the
Victory gained the coast of Barbary, the
wind, which had blown for several days
from the west, shifted to the eastward, and
a fresh breeze sprung up; she therefore
changed her course, and stood back again
for Gibraltar, where she arrived early in the
morning. She then lay-to in the bay without
anchoring, and the boats were immediately

sent on shore for the wounded; who were all brought off by noon, except five of the worst cases who could not be removed.[6] In the afternoon the Victory and Bellisle sailed from Gibraltar Bay, and passed through the Straits during the night of the 4th. The next day at noon they joined the squadron under the command of Admiral COLLINGWOOD, then cruising off Cadiz; from which they parted company the same evening, and pursued their course together for England.

WHEN the Victory had proceeded some weeks on her voyage, adverse winds and tempestuous weather having prolonged the passage much beyond the period that is generally expected, it was thought proper to draw off the spirit from the cask containing Lord NELSON's Body, and renew it; and this was done twice. On these occasions brandy

[6] OF the Victory's wounded, three died before she reached Gibraltar, one on the day of her arrival there, and another at the naval hospital at that place a few days afterwards: all the rest got well on board except the five left at Gibraltar, and five others not perfectly recovered from their wounds in January following; when the Victory being put out of commission at Chatham, they were sent to the Sussex hospital-ship at Sheerness.

was used in the proportion of two-thirds to one of spirit of wine.

AT length the Victory arrived at Spithead, after a tedious passage of nearly five weeks from Gibraltar: and as no instructions respecting HIS LORDSHIP's Remains were received at Portsmouth while the ship remained there, and orders being transmitted to Captain HARDY for her to proceed to the Nore, the Surgeon represented to him the necessity of examining the state of the Body; common report giving reason to believe that it was intended to lie in state at Greenwich Hospital, and to be literally exposed to the public. On the 11th of December therefore, the day on which the Victory sailed from Spithead for the Nore, Lord NELSON's Body was taken from the cask in which it had been kept since the day after his death. On inspecting it externally, it exhibited a state of perfect preservation, without being in the smallest degree offensive. There were, however, some appearances that induced the Surgeon to examine the condition of the bowels; which were found to be much decayed, and likely in a short time to communicate the process of putrefaction to the rest of the Body: the parts already injured were therefore removed. It was at this time that the fatal ball was discovered: it had passed through the spine, and lodged in the muscles of the back, towards the right side, and a little below the shoulder-blade. A very considerable portion of the gold-lace, pad, and lining of the epaulette, with a piece of the coat, was found attached to the ball: the lace of the epaulette was as firmly so, as if it had been inserted into the metal while in a state of fusion.[7]

THE following is the professional Report on HIS LORDSHIP's wound and death, made by the Surgeon on this occasion:

"*His Majesty's Ship Victory, at Sea,*
11th December, 1805

"ABOUT the middle of the action with the Combined Fleets on the 21st of October last, the late illustrious Com-

---

[7] THE ball was *not* fired from a rifle piece.

mander in Chief Lord NELSON was mortally wounded in the left breast by a
musket-ball, supposed to be fired from
the mizen-top of La Redoutable French
ship of the line, which the Victory fell
on board of early in the battle. HIS
LORDSHIP was in the act of turning on
the quarter-deck with his face towards
the Enemy, when he received his wound:
he instantly fell; and was carried to the
cockpit, where he lived about two
hours.[8] On being brought below, he
complained of acute pain about the sixth
or seventh dorsal vertebra, and of privation of sense and motion of the body and
inferior extremities. His respiration was
short and difficult; pulse weak, small,
and irregular. He frequently declared
his back was shot through, that he felt
every instant a gush of blood within his
breast, and that he had sensations which
indicated to him the approach of death.

[8] IT was not deemed necessary to insert in this Report
the precise time which HIS LORDSHIP survived his
wound. This, as before stated, was in reality two hours
and three quarters.

In the course of an hour his pulse became indistinct, and was gradually lost in the arm. His extremities and forehead became soon afterwards cold. He retained his wonted energy of mind, and exercise of his faculties, till the last moment of his existence; and when the victory as signal as decisive was announced to him, he expressed his pious acknowledgments, and heart-felt satisfaction at the glorious event, in the most emphatic language. He then delivered his last orders with his usual precision, and in a few minutes afterwards expired without a struggle.

"Course and site of the Ball, as ascertained since death.

"THE ball struck the fore part of HIS LORDSHIP'S epaulette; and entered the left shoulder immediately before the processus acromion scapulæ, which it slightly fractured. It then descended obliquely into the thorax, fracturing the second and third ribs: and after penetrating the left lobe of the lungs, and

Fig 1.

a   Piece of the Coat
b   The Ball
ccc Depressions in the Ball by striking against Bone

d Gold Lace fixed in the Ball
e Piece of the Silk pad
ff Lace of the Bullion

Fig 2.

The Ball,

which mortally wounded

The **LAMENTED NELSON** of

Glorious & Immortal Memory.

Pub. as the Act directs by W. Beatty 1st Octr. 1806.

dividing in its passage a large branch of the pulmonary artery, it entered the left side of the spine between the sixth and seventh dorsal vertebræ, fractured the left transverse process of the sixth dorsal vertebra, wounded the medulla spinalis, and fracturing the right transverse process of the seventh vertebra, made its way from the right side of the spine, directing its course through the muscles of the back; and lodged therein, about two inches below the inferior angle of the right scapula. On removing the ball, a portion of the gold-lace and pad of the epaulette, together with a small piece of His Lordship's coat, was found firmly attached to it.[9]

"W. Beatty."

[9] Fig. 1. in the annexed Plate represents the Ball in the exact state in which it was extracted. Drawn by Mr. W.E. Devis, who was then on board the Victory.

Fig. 2. (drawn also by Mr. Devis) shews the Ball in its present state; as set in crystal by Mr. Yonge, and presented to the Writer of this Narrative by Sir Thomas Hardy.

The Ball, in perforating the epaulette, passed through many of the silk cords supporting the bullions, and through the pad and a doubling of silk besides; as the bag

THE Remains were wrapped in cotton vestments, and rolled from head to foot with bandages of the same material, in the ancient mode of embalming. The Body was then put into a leaden coffin, filled with brandy holding in solution camphor and myrrh.[1] This coffin was inclosed in a wooden one, and placed in the after-part of HIS LORDSHIP's cabin; where it remained till the 21st of December, when an order was received from the Admiralty for the removal of the Body. The coffin that had been made from the mainmast of the French Commander's ship L'Orient, and presented to HIS LORDSHIP by his friend Captain HOLLOWELL, after the battle of the Nile, being then received on board, the leaden coffin was opened, and the Body taken

of the pad was composed of yellow silk. This circumstance militates strongly against an opinion entertained by some, that silk possesses in an eminent degree the power of resisting the force, or arresting the velocity, of a musket or pistol ball.

[1] THE stock of spirit of wine on board was exhausted; and from the sound state of the Body, brandy was judged sufficient for its preservation.

out; when it was found still in most
excellent condition, and completely
plastic. The features were somewhat
tumid, from absorption of the spirit; but
on using friction with a napkin, they
resumed in a great degree their natural
character. All the Officers of the ship,
and several of HIS LORDSHIP's friends, as
well as some of Captain HARDY's, who
had come on board the Victory that day
from the shore, were present at the time
of the Body's being removed from the
leaden coffin; and witnessed its unde-
cayed state after a lapse of two months
since death, which excited the surprise
of all who beheld it. This was the last
time the mortal part of the lamented
Hero was seen by human eyes; as the
Body, after being dressed in a shirt,
stockings, uniform small-clothes and
waistcoat, neck-cloth, and night-cap,
was then placed in the shell made from
L'Orient's mast, and covered with the
shrouding. This was inclosed in a leaden
coffin; which was soldered up immediately, and put into another wooden

shell: in which manner it was sent out of the Victory into Commissioner GREY's yacht, which was hauled alongside for that purpose. In this vessel the revered Remains were conveyed to Greenwich Hospital; attended by the Reverend Doctor SCOTT, and Messrs. TYSON and WHITBY.

LORD NELSON had often talked with Captain HARDY on the subject of his being killed in battle, which appeared indeed to be a favourite topic of conversation with him. He was always prepared to lay down his life in the service of his Country; and whenever it should please Providence to remove him from this world, it was the most ambitious wish of his soul to die in the fight, and in the very hour of a great and signal victory. In this he was gratified: his end was glorious; and he died as he had lived, one of the greatest among men.

THE following Prayer, found in HIS LORDSHIP's memorandum-book,—and written with his own hand on the night of his leaving Merton, at one of the places where he changed horses (supposed to be Guildford) on his way to join the Victory at Portsmouth,—is highly illustrative of those sentiments of combined piety and patriotic heroism with which he was inspired:

"Friday Night, 13th September.

"FRIDAY night, at half past ten, drove from dear, dear Merton, where I left all which I hold dear in this world, to go to serve my King and Country. May the great GOD whom I adore, enable me to fulfil the expectations of my Country! and if it is His good pleasure that I should return, my thanks will never cease being offered up to the throne of His mercy. But if it is His good providence to cut short my days upon earth, I bow with the greatest submission; relying that He will protect those, so dear to me, that I may leave behind. His will be done!

"AMEN, amen, amen."

His Lordship had on several occasions told Captain Hardy, that if he should fall in battle in a foreign climate, he wished his body to be conveyed to England; and that if his Country should think proper to inter him at the public expence, he wished to be buried in Saint Paul's, as well as that his monument should be erected there. He explained his reasons for preferring Saint Paul's to Westminster Abbey, which were rather curious: he said that he remembered hearing it stated as an old tradition when he was a boy, that Westminster Abbey was built on a spot where once existed a deep morass; and he thought it likely that the lapse of time would reduce the ground on which it now stands to its primitive state of a swamp, without leaving a trace of the Abbey. He added, that his actual observations confirmed the probability of this event. He also repeated to Captain Hardy several times during the last two years of his life: "Should I be killed, Hardy, and my Country not bury me, you know what to do with me;" meaning that his body was in that case to be laid by the side of his Father's, in his native village of Burnham Thorpe in Norfolk: and this, as has been before mentioned (in page 49), he adverted to in his last moments.

AN opinion has been very generally entertained, that Lord NELSON's state of health, and supposed infirmities arising from his former wounds and hard services, precluded the probability of his long surviving the battle of Trafalgar, had he fortunately escaped the Enemy's shot: but the Writer of this can assert that HIS LORDSHIP's health was uniformly good, with the exception of some slight attacks of indisposition arising from accidental causes; and which never continued above two or three days, nor confined him in any degree with respect to either exercise or regimen:[2] and during the last twelve

---

[2] THESE complaints were the consequence of indigestion, brought on by writing for several hours together. HIS LORDSHIP had one of these attacks from that cause a few days before the battle, but on resuming his accustomed exercise he got rid of it. This attack alarmed him, as he attributed it to sudden and violent spasm; but it was merely an unpleasant symptom (*globus hystericus*) attending indigestion.

months of his life, he complained only three times in this way. It is true, that HIS LORDSHIP, about the meridian of life, had been subject to frequent fits of the gout: which disease however, as well as his constitutional tendency to it, he totally overcame by abstaining for the space of nearly two years from animal food, and wine and all other fermented drink; confining his diet to vegetables, and commonly milk and water. And it is also a fact, that early in life, when he first went to sea, he left off the use of salt, which he then believed to be the sole cause of scurvy, and never took it afterwards with his food.

HIS LORDSHIP used a great deal of exercise, generally walking on deck six or seven hours in the day. He always rose early, for the most part shortly after day-break. He breakfasted in summer about six, and at seven in winter: and if not occupied in reading or writing dispatches, or examining into the details of the Fleet, he walked on the quarter-deck the greater part of the forenoon; going down to his cabin occasionally to commit to paper such incidents or reflections as occurred to him during that time, and as might be hereafter useful to the service of his country. He dined generally about half past two o'clock. At his table there were seldom less than eight or nine persons, consisting of the different Officers of the ship: and when the weather and the service permitted, he very often had several of the Admirals and Captains in the Fleet to dine with him; who were mostly invited by signal, the rotation of seniority being commonly observed by HIS LORDSHIP in these invitations. At dinner he was alike affable and attentive to every one: he ate very sparingly himself; the liver and wing of a fowl, and a small plate of macaroni, in general composing his meal, during which he occasionally took a glass of Champagne. He never exceeded four glasses of wine after dinner, and seldom drank three; and even these were diluted with either Bristol or common water.

FEW men subject to the vicissitudes of a naval life, equalled HIS LORDSHIP in an habitual systematic mode of living. He possessed such a wonderful activity of mind, as even prevented him from taking ordinary

repose, seldom enjoying two hours of unin-
terrupted sleep; and on several occasions he
did not quit the deck during the whole
night. At these times he took no pains to
protect himself from the effects of wet, or
the night-air; wearing only a thin great
coat: and he has frequently, after having his
clothes wet through with rain, refused to
have them changed, saying that the leather
waistcoat which he wore over his flannel
one would secure him from complaint. He
seldom wore boots, and was consequently
very liable to have his feet wet. When this
occurred he has often been known to go
down to his cabin, throw off his shoes, and
walk on the carpet in his stockings for the
purpose of drying the feet of them. He chose
rather to adopt this uncomfortable expe-
dient, than to give his servants the trouble
of assisting him to put on fresh stockings;
which, from his having only one hand, he
could not himself conveniently effect.

FROM these circumstances it may be in-
ferred, that though Lord NELSON's constitu-
tion was not of that kind which is generally
denominated strong, yet it was not very

susceptible of complaint from the common occasional causes of disease necessarily attending a naval life. The only bodily pain which HIS LORDSHIP felt in consequence of his many wounds, was a slight rheumatic affection of the stump of his amputated arm on any sudden variation in the state of the weather; which is generally experienced by those who have the misfortune to lose a limb after the middle age. HIS LORDSHIP usually predicted an alteration in the weather with as much certainty from feeling transient pains in this stump, as he could by his marine barometer; from the indications of which latter he kept a diary of the atmospheric changes, which was written with his own hand.

HIS LORDSHIP had lost his right eye by a contusion which he received at the siege of Calvi, in the island of Corsica. The vision of the other was likewise considerably impaired: he always therefore wore a green shade over his forehead, to defend this eye from the effect of strong light; but as he was in the habit of looking much through a glass while on deck, there is little doubt, that had he lived a few years longer, and continued at sea, he would have lost his sight totally.

THE Surgeon had, on the occasion of opening HIS LORDSHIP'S Body, an opportunity of acquiring an accurate knowledge of the sound and healthy state of the thoracic and abdominal viscera, none of which appeared to have ever been the seat of inflammation or disease. There were no morbid indications to be seen; other than those unavoidably attending the human body six weeks after death, even under circumstances more favourable to its preservation. The heart was small, and dense in its substance; its valves, pericardium, and the large vessels, were sound, and firm in their structure. The lungs were sound, and free from adhesions. The liver was very small, in its colour natural, firm in its texture, and every way free from the smallest appearance of disorganization. The stomach, as well as the spleen and other abdominal contents, was alike free from the traces of disease. Indeed all the vital parts were so perfectly healthy in their appearance, and so small, that they resembled more those of a youth, than of a man who had attained his forty-seventh year; which state of the body, associated with habits of life favourable to health, gives every reason to believe that HIS LORDSHIP might have lived to a great age.

THE immediate cause of HIS LORDSHIP'S death was a wound of the left pulmonary artery, which poured out its blood into the cavity of the chest. The quantity of blood thus effused did not appear to be very great; but as the hemorrhage was from a vessel so near the heart, and the blood was consequently lost in a very short time, it produced death sooner than would have been effected by a larger quantity of blood lost from an artery in a more remote part of the body. The injury done to the spine must of itself have proved mortal, but HIS LORDSHIP might perhaps have survived this alone for two or three days; though his existence protracted even for that short period would have been miserable to himself, and highly distressing to the feelings of all around him.

W. BEATTY.

APPENDIX

Instructions issued by Lord Nelson to the
Admirals and Captains of the Fleet,
several days previous to the Battle

Victory, off Cadiz, 10th of

October, 1805

GENERAL MEMORANDUM *sent to the Commanders of*
Ships

THINKING it almost impossible to bring a
Fleet of forty sail of the line into a line of battle
in variable winds, thick weather, and other
circumstances which must occur, without such
a loss of time that the opportunity would
probably be lost of bringing the Enemy to
battle in such a manner as to make the business
decisive, I have therefore made up my mind to
keep the Fleet in that position of sailing, with
the exception of the First and Second in Com-

J.W. Lewis pinx.

E. Scriven sculp.

LORD VISCOUNT NELSON

Duke of Bronte &c. &c. &c.

In the Dress he wore, when he received his Mortal Wound
21st Oct. 1805.

Published by Cadell & Davies. Nov. 17. 1806.

mand, that the order of sailing is to be the order of battle: placing the Fleet in two lines, of sixteen ships each, with an advanced squadron of eight of the fastest-sailing two-decked ships; which will always make, if wanted, a line of twenty-four sail, on whichever line the Commander in Chief may direct.

THE Second in Command will, after my intentions are made known to him, have the entire direction of his line; to make the attack upon the Enemy, and to follow up the blow until they are captured or destroyed.

IF the Enemy's Fleet should be seen to windward in line of battle, and that the two lines and advanced squadron could fetch them, they will probably be so extended that their van could not succour their rear: I should therefore probably make the Second in Command's signal to lead through about their twelfth ship from their rear; or wherever he could fetch, if not able to get so far advanced. My line would lead through about their centre: and the advanced squadron to cut three or four ships ahead of their centre, so as to ensure getting at their Commander in Chief, on whom every effort must be made to capture.

THE whole impression of the British Fleet must be, to overpower from two or three ships ahead of the Commander in Chief (supposed to be in the centre) to the rear of their Fleet.

I WILL suppose twenty sail of the Enemy's line to be untouched: it must be some time before they could perform a manœuvre to bring their force compact to attack any part of the British Fleet engaged, or to succour their own ships; which indeed would be impossible, without mixing with the ships engaged. The Enemy's Fleet is supposed to consist of forty-six sail of the line; British, forty:[1] if either is less, only a proportional number of Enemy's ships are to be cut off; British to be one-fourth superior to the Enemy cut off.

SOMETHING must be left to chance: nothing is sure in a sea-fight, beyond all others; shot will carry away masts and yards of friends as well as foes: but I look with confidence to a victory before the van of the Enemy could succour their rear; and then that the British Fleet would most of them be ready to receive their twenty sail of the line, or to pursue them should they endeavour to make off.

---

[1] WITH such an inferiority of force as his, HIS LORDSHIP confidently expected not only to gain a decisive victory, but (to use his own favourite phrase) "completely to *annihilate the Enemy's Fleet!*"

IF the van of the Enemy tack, the captured ships must run to leeward of the British Fleet: if the Enemy wear, the British must place themselves between the Enemy and captured, and disabled British ships: and should the Enemy close, I have no fear for the result.

THE Second in Command will, in all possible things, direct the movements of his line, by keeping them so compact as the nature of the circumstances will admit. Captains are to look to their particular line as their rallying-point; but in case signals cannot be seen or clearly understood, no Captain can do very wrong if he places his ship alongside that of an Enemy.

PLAN of the intended attack from to-windward, the Enemy in line of battle ready to receive an attack:

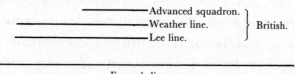

The divisions of the British Fleet will be brought nearly within gun-shot of the Enemy's centre. The signal will be made for the lee line to bear up together; to set all their sail, even studding-sails, in order to get as quickly as possible to the Enemy's line; and to cut through, beginning from the twelfth ship from the Enemy's rear. Some ships may not get through their exact place, but they will always be at hand to assist their friends. If any are thrown in the rear of the Enemy, they will effectually complete the business of twelve sail of the Enemy.

SHOULD the Enemy wear together, or bear up and sail large, still the twelve ships composing in the first position the Enemy's rear, are to be the object of attack of the lee line, unless otherwise directed by the Commander in Chief; which is scarcely to be expected; as the entire management of the lee line, after the intentions of the Commander in Chief are signified, is intended to be left to the Admiral commanding that line.

THE remainder of the Enemy's Fleet, thirty-four sail, are to be left to the management of the Commander in Chief; who will endeavour to take care that the movements of the Second in Command are as little interrupted as possible.

NELSON AND BRONTE.

By COMMAND OF THE VICE ADMIRAL.
JNO. SCOTT.

AUTHENTIC NARRATIVE

OF THE

Death

OF

LORD NELSON:

WITH

THE CIRCUMSTANCES PRECEDING, ATTENDING, AND
SUBSEQUENT TO, THAT EVENT;

THE

PROFESSIONAL REPORT

ON HIS LORDSHIP'S WOUND;

AND

SEVERAL INTERESTING ANECDOTES.

BY WILLIAM BEATTY, M.D.

... to the Victory in the Battle of Trafalgar, and now Physician to the Fleet under the
Command of the Earl of St. Vincent, K. B. &c. &c. &c.

LONDON:

PRINTED BY T. DAVISON, WHITE-FRIARS;
FOR T. CADELL AND W. DAVIES, IN THE STRAND.

1807.

*The following interesting Extracts are faithfully
copied from* His Lordship's *Memorandum
Book, written entirely in his own hand*

———

SATURDAY, September 14th, 1805. At six
o'clock arrived at Portsmouth; and having
arranged all my business, embarked at the
bathing-machines with Mr. ROSE and Mr.
CANNING, who dined with me. At two got on
board the Victory, at St. Helen's.

WEDNESDAY, Sept. 25th, 1805. Light airs
southerly. Saw the rock of Lisbon S.S.E. ten
leagues. At sunset the Captain of the Constance
came on board, and sent my letters for England
to Lisbon, and wrote to Captain SUTTON[2] and
the Consul. The Enemy's Fleet had not left
Cadiz the 18th of this month, therefore I yet
hope they will wait my arrival.

SATURDAY, Sept. 28th, 1805. Fresh breezes at
N.N.W. At day-light bore up, and made sail.
At nine saw the Ætna cruising. At noon saw

[2] OF his Majesty's ship Amphion, then in the Tagus.

eighteen sail. Nearly calm. In the evening joined the Fleet under Vice Admiral COLLINGWOOD. Saw the Enemy's Fleet in Cadiz, amounting to thirty-five or thirty-six sail of the line.

SUNDAY, Sept. 29th. Fine weather. Gave out the necessary orders for the Fleet. Sent Euryalus to watch the Enemy with the Hydra off Cadiz.

WEDNESDAY, October 9th. Fresh breezes easterly. Received an account from BLACKWOOD, that the French ships had all bent their top-gallant-sails. Sent the Pickle to him, with orders to keep a good look-out. Sent Admiral COLLINGWOOD the NELSON truth.[3] At night wind westerly.

MONDAY, Oct. 14th. Fine weather: westerly wind. Sent Amphion to Gibraltar and Algiers. Enemy at the harbour's mouth. Placed Defence and Agamemnon from seven to ten leagues west of Cadiz; and Mars and Colossus five leagues east of the Fleet, whose station is from fifteen to twenty west of Cadiz: and by this chain I hope to have a constant communication with the frigates off Cadiz.

---

[3] IT is presumed that HIS LORDSHIP here meant the preceding Instructions, which were transmitted the next day to the whole Fleet.

WEDNESDAY, Oct. 16th. Moderate breezes westerly. All the forenoon employed forming the Fleet into the order of sailing. At noon fresh breezes W.S.W. and squally. In the evening fresh gales. The Enemy as before, by signal from Weazle.

THURSDAY, Oct. 17th. Moderate breezes north-westerly. Sent the Donegal to Gibraltar, to get a ground-tier of casks. Received accounts by the Diligent storeship, that Sir RICHARD STRACHAN was supposed in sight of the French Rochefort squadron; which I hope is true.

FRIDAY, Oct. 18th. Fine weather: wind easterly. The Combined Fleets cannot have finer weather to put to sea.

SATURDAY, Oct. 19th. Fine weather: wind easterly. At half past nine the Mars, being one of the look-out ships, made the signal that the Enemy were coming out of port. Made the signal for a general chace S.E. Wind at south; Cadiz bearing E.S.E. by compass, distance sixteen leagues. At three the Colossus made the signal that the Enemy's Fleet was at sea. In the evening made the signal to observe my motions during the night; for the Britannia, Prince, and Dreadnought, to take stations as most convenient, and for Mars, Orion, Belleisle, Leviathan, Bellerophon, and Polyphemus, to go ahead during the night, and to carry a light, standing for the Straits' mouth.

SUNDAY, Oct. 20th. Fresh breezes S.S.W., and rainy. Communicated with Phœbe, Defence, and Colossus, who saw near forty sail of ships of war outside of Cadiz yesterday evening; but the wind being southerly, they could not get to the mouth of the Straits. We were between Trafalgar and Cape Spartel. The frigates made the signal that they saw nine sail outside the harbour. Sent the frigates instructions for their guidance; and placed the Defence, Colossus, and Mars, between me and the frigates. At noon fresh gales, and heavy rain: Cadiz N.E. nine leagues. In the afternoon Captain BLACKWOOD telegraphed that the Enemy seemed determined to go to the westward;—and *that* they shall *not* do, if in the power of NELSON AND BRONTE to prevent them. At five telegraphed Captain BLACKWOOD, that I relied upon his keeping sight of the Enemy. At five o'clock Naiad made the signal for thirty-one sail of the Enemy N.N.E. The frigates and look-out ship kept sight of the Enemy most admirably all night, and told me by signal which tack they were upon. At eight we wore, and stood to the S.W.; and at four wore and stood to the N.E.

MONDAY, Oct. 21st. At day-light saw
Enemy's Combined Fleets from east to E.S.E.
Bore away. Made the signal for order of sailing,
and to prepare for battle. The Enemy with their
heads to the southward. At seven the Enemy
wearing in succession.

*Then follow the Prayer and Codicil already inserted
in pages* 19, 20 *and* 21 *of the Narrative, which
conclude* His Lordship's *manuscript*